Thelma &
Bubbette

Published by Willow Creek Press, Inc.
P.O. Box 147, Minocqua, Wisconsin 54548

All photography © Christina Bynum-Breaux
Design by Sara Olson

Printed in China

Thelma & Bubbette

The Ultimate Girlfriend Book

WILLOW CREEK PRESS®

Photography by Christina Bynum-Breaux

GIGI: *So maybe his grandma died or maybe he lost my number or is out of town or got hit by a cab...*

ALEX: *Or maybe he is not interested in seeing you again.*

—HE'S JUST NOT THAT INTO YOU

HELEN: [Crying] Why are you smiling?

ANNIE: *It's just… it's the first time I've ever seen you look ugly… and that makes me kind of happy.*

—*BRIDESMAIDS*

DOUG: *Fashion is not about utility.*
An accessory is merely a piece of iconography
used to express individual identity.

LILLY: *Oooh! And it's pretty!*

DOUG: *That too.*

—THE DEVIL WEARS PRADA

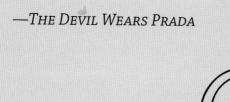

VIVIAN: *You're late.*

EDWARD: *You're stunning.*

VIVIAN: *You're forgiven.*

—PRETTY WOMAN

LUCY: *Ok, you can wipe the doe-eyed-Bambi-watching-her-mother-get-shot-and-strapped-to-the-back-of-a-van look from your face.*

—13 GOING ON 30

SHELBY: *Well, we went skinny dipping and we did things that frightened the fish.*

—STEEL MAGNOLIAS

THELMA: You said you 'n' me was gonna get out of town and for once just really let our hair down. Well darlin', look out 'cause my hair is comin' down!

—THELMA & LOUISE

HOLLY: *A girl can't read that sort of thing without her lipstick.*

—*BREAKFAST AT TIFFANY'S*

CLAIREE: *The only thing that separates us from the animals is our ability to accessorize.*

—STEEL MAGNOLIAS

ANDIE: *Well, not nothing.*
I mean, I kissed him...

IONA: *Anywhere interesting?*

—PRETTY IN PINK

SAM: *Maybe this whole relationship is just better off in cyberspace.*

—A CINDERELLA STORY

ROSE: *It's so unfair.*

RUTH: *Of course it's unfair. We're women. Our choices are never easy.*

—*TITANIC*

BOBBY RAY: *You can take the girl out of the honky tonk, but you can't take the honky tonk out of the girl.*

—*Sweet Home Alabama*

KAT: *Oh wait... was that...*
did your hairline just recede?

—10 THINGS I HATE ABOUT YOU

SUGAR: *I don't care how rich he is,*
as long as he has a yacht,
his own private railroad car,
and his own toothpaste.

—SOME LIKE IT HOT

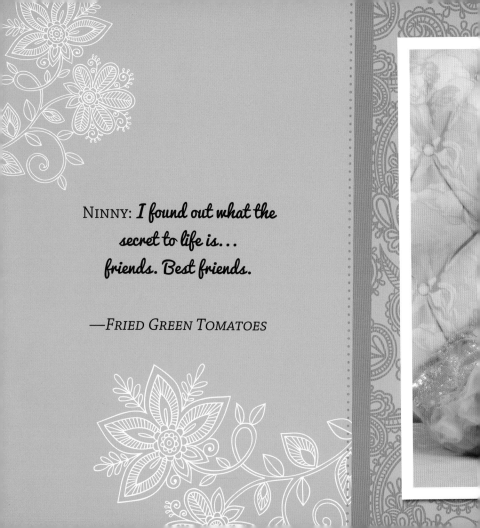

NINNY: *I found out what the secret to life is... friends. Best friends.*

—FRIED GREEN TOMATOES

IAN: Why are you trying so hard to fit in when you are born to stand out?

—WHAT A GIRL WANTS

TRUVY: *In a good shoe, I wear a size six,*
but a seven feels so good, I buy a size eight.

—STEEL MAGNOLIAS

JOHNNY:
Nobody puts Baby in a corner.

—*DIRTY DANCING*

VIC: *Your hair should make a statement.*

GRACIE: *As long as it doesn't say,*
"Thank you very much for the Country Music Award!"

—MISS CONGENIALITY

ANDY: *I love that. Will that fit me?*

NIGEL: *A little Crisco and some fishing wire and we'll be in business.*

—THE DEVIL WEARS PRADA

CC BLOOM: *But enough about me, let's talk about you... what do YOU think of me?*

—*BEACHES*

BIANCA: *There's a difference between like and love. Because, I like my Skechers, but I love my Prada backpack.*

CHASTITY: *But I love my Sketchers.*

BIANCA: *That's because you don't have a Prada backpack.*

—*10 THINGS I HATE ABOUT YOU*

JOCELYN: *Everybody's rooting for you to fail.*
That's what makes it fun.

—WHAT A GIRL WANTS

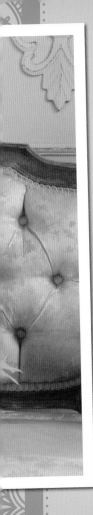

FIONA: *I am very, very, very, very upset about this.*

BRIANNA: *You don't look upset.*

FIONA: *Oh, it's the Botox. I can't show emotion for another hour and a half.*

—*A CINDERELLA STORY*

MIA: *I don't want something I need.*
I want something I want—something pretty.

—*LOVE ACTUALLY*

SHELBY: *Relax! You can't screw up her hair.*
Just tease it and make it look like a brown football helmet.

—STEEL MAGNOLIAS

CHER: *Do you prefer "fashion victim" or "ensembly challenged"?*

—CLUELESS

LUCY: *Nothing beats a first kiss.*

—*50 FIRST DATES*

DUCKIE: *This is a really volcanic ensemble you're wearing, it's really marvelous!*

—PRETTY IN PINK

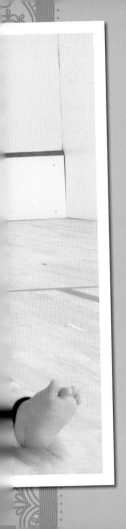

TAI: *Cher, I don't want to do this anymore.*
And my buns, they don't feel nothin' like steel.

—*CLUELESS*

JESSICA: *I'll be the envy of every girl at the prom.*
Not like that was in jeopardy or anything.

—THE HOT CHICK

PENNY: *Oh, come on, ladies. God wouldn't have given you maracas if He didn't want you to shake 'em!*

—DIRTY DANCING

JOSIE: *The right guy, he's out there. I'm just not gonna go kiss a whole bunch of losers to get to him.*

ANITA: *Yeah, but you know what? Sometimes kissing losers can be a really fun diversion.*

—*NEVER BEEN KISSED*